Real Science-4

CHEMISTRY

Level I

Rebecca W. Keller, Ph.D.

Cover design: David Keller
Opening page: David Keller
Illustrations: Rebecca W. Keller, Ph.D.

Copyright ©2004, 2005, 2007, 2008, 2009, 2010, 2011 Gravitas Publications, Inc.

Level I Chemistry Student Textbook

ISBN # 978-1-936114-25-2

Published by Gravitas Publications, Inc.
4116 Jackie Road SE, Suite 101
Rio Rancho, NM 87124
www.gravitaspublications.com

Illustrations
Chapter 9, 9.1: Art Today
Chapter 10: All molecular coordinates were provided by the Brookhaven Protein Data Bank.

Front cover: water molecule showing both the bonding of two hydrogens to one oxygen and the van der Waals radii of the atoms
Back cover, inside title page: L-alanine molecule—one of the amino acids

Special thanks to Susan Searles for copyediting and review of the manuscript. Also, I'd like to thank the Keller kids (Kimberly, Chris, and Katy), the Chesebrough kids (Sam and Ben), and the Megill kids (Lorien, Lee, Joshua, and Joseph) for critical evaluation of the text. Finally, I'd like to thank Lina and Lillian McEwan for valuable input.

GRAVITAS

Contents

The Periodic Table of Elements

Noble gases

Halogens

Alkali metals
Alkaline earth metals

Metals
Non-metals

Metalloids
Synthetic elements (unconfirmed)

Transition metals

1 H Hydrogen 1.0079																	2 He Helium 4.003
3 Li Lithium 6.941	4 Be Beryllium 9.0122											5 B Boron 10.811	6 C Carbon 12.011	7 N Nitrogen 14.0067	8 O Oxygen 15.9994	9 F Fluorine 18.9984	10 Ne Neon 20.1797
11 Na Sodium 22.9898	12 Mg Magnesium 24.3050											13 Al Aluminum 26.9815	14 Si Silicon 28.0855	15 P Phosphorus 30.9738	16 S Sulfur 32.066	17 Cl Chlorine 35.4527	18 Ar Argon 39.948
19 K Potassium 39.0983	20 Ca Calcium 40.078	21 Sc Scandium 44.9559	22 Ti Titanium 47.867	23 V Vanadium 50.9415	24 Cr Chromium 51.9961	25 Mn Manganese 54.9380	26 Fe Iron 55.847	27 Co Cobalt 58.9332	28 Ni Nickel 58.693	29 Cu Copper 63.546	30 Zn Zinc 65.38	31 Ga Gallium 69.723	32 Ge Germanium 72.63	33 As Arsenic 74.9216	34 Se Selenium 78.96	35 Br Bromine 79.904	36 Kr Krypton 83.80
37 Rb Rubidium 85.4678	38 Sr Strontium 87.62	39 Y Yttrium 88.9059	40 Zr Zirconium 91.224	41 Nb Niobium 92.9064	42 Mo Molybdenum 95.96	43 Tc Technetium (98)	44 Ru Ruthenium 101.07	45 Rh Rhodium 102.9055	46 Pd Palladium 106.42	47 Ag Silver 107.8682	48 Cd Cadmium 112.411	49 In Indium 114.82	50 Sn Tin 118.710	51 Sb Antimony 121.757	52 Te Tellurium 127.60	53 I Iodine 126.9045	54 Xe Xenon 131.29
55 Cs Cesium 132.9054	56 Ba Barium 137.327	57 *La Lanthanum 138.9055	72 Hf Hafnium 178.49	73 Ta Tantalum 180.9479	74 W Tungsten 183.84	75 Re Rhenium 186.207	76 Os Osmium 190.2	77 Ir Iridium 192.22	78 Pt Platinum 195.08	79 Au Gold 196.9666	80 Hg Mercury 200.59	81 Tl Thallium 204.3833	82 Pb Lead 207.2	83 Bi Bismuth 208.9804	84 Po Polonium (209)	85 At Astatine (210)	86 Rn Radon (222)
87 Fr Francium (223)	88 Ra Radium 226.0254	89 **Ac Actinium 227.0278	104 Rf Rutherfordium 261	105 Db Dubnium 262.11	106 Sg Seaborgium 263	107 Bh Bohrium 264.12	108 Hs Hassium 269.13	109 Mt Meitnerium 266	110 Ds Darmstadtium (269)	111 Rg Roentgenium (272)	112 Cp Copernicium (277)	113 Uut Ununtrium (284)	114 Uuq Ununquadium (285)	115 Uup Ununpentium (288)	116 Uuh Ununhexium (289)	117 Uus Ununseptium (289)	118 Uuo Ununoctium (293)

58 Ce Cerium 140.116	59 Pr Praseodymium 140.9076	60 Nd Neodymium 144.24	61 Pm Promethium (145)	62 Sm Samarium 150.36	63 Eu Europium 151.964	64 Gd Gadolinium 157.25	65 Tb Terbium 158.9253	66 Dy Dysprosium 162.50	67 Ho Holmium 164.9303	68 Er Erbium 167.26	69 Tm Thulium 168.9342	70 Yb Ytterbium 173.054	71 Lu Lutetium 174.967
90 Th Thorium 232.0381	91 Pa Protactinium 231.0359	92 U Uranium 238.0289	93 Np Neptunium 237.0482	94 Pu Plutonium (244)	95 Am Americium (243)	96 Cm Curium (247)	97 Bk Berkelium (247)	98 Cf Californium (251)	99 Es Einsteinium (252)	100 Fm Fermium (257)	101 Md Mendelevium (258)	102 No Nobelium (259)	103 Lr Lawrencium (260)

*The lanthinide series: Elements 58–71

**The actinide series: Elements 90–103

http://www.gravitaspublications.com

Chapter 1 Matter

Atomic number

1

H

Hydrogen

1.0079

Symbol

Name

Atomic weight

Hydrogen has only one proton and no neutrons.

1.1 Introduction

What is chemistry? Have you ever wondered what the world and the objects in the world are made of? What is water exactly? Why do ice cubes float? What are our hair and skin made of? Why is a marble hard but a jellyfish soft?

All of these questions, and others like them, begin the inquiry into that branch of science called chemistry.

Chemistry is the study of matter which is a general term for what forms all living and nonliving things.

Chemistry is concerned mainly with the properties of matter. All of the items we encounter on a daily basis are made of matter.

Balloons are made of matter.

Pancakes are made of matter.

Baseballs are made of matter. Even our bodies are made of matter. But what makes up matter?

1.2 Atoms

The fundamental building blocks of matter are atoms (a´-təms). The word atom comes from the Greek word *atomos*, which means "uncuttable." During the 5th century b.c., the Greek philosophers proposed the idea that there must be some smallest uncuttable units of matter. They called these units atoms.

Today we know that atoms are composed of even smaller particles called protons (prō'-tänz), neutrons (nü'-tränz), and electrons (i-lek'-tränz).

Protons and neutrons are roughly equal in size, but electrons are very much smaller than both protons and neutrons. Protons, neutrons, and electrons are all much smaller than an atom.

Proton

Neutron

Electron

Helium Atom

Protons and neutrons combine to form the central core or nucleus (nü'-klē-əs) of an atom. The electrons occupy the space surrounding the nucleus. This space is sometimes called the electron cloud.

The number of electrons in an atom always equals the number of protons. Notice that in the helium (hē'-lē-um) atom there are two protons and two electrons. Sometimes the number of protons also equals the number of neutrons, as with helium, but this is not always true.

Most of the space of an atom is actually filled up by the electron cloud. The central core of an atom takes up only a very small part of the total space.

neutrons

electrons

protons

On the other hand, almost all of the mass of the atom is in the protons and neutrons in the nucleus. The electrons weigh almost nothing compared to the nucleus, yet they take up all the space!

1.3 Periodic table

All of the atoms that make up the world are known. They are called chemical elements or just elements (e'-lə-mənts). Early in the 19th century, a total of 55 chemical elements were known, and many more were being discovered. Their properties were very different from each other, and it was difficult to organize them. In 1867, Dmitri Mendeleev (dmē'-trē men-də-lā'-əf) organized the elements into what is now called the periodic table of elements.

In today's periodic table, the elements are arranged horizontally from left to right in order of increasing atomic number. The atomic number is the number of protons in the nucleus of each atom. For example, carbon has an atomic number of 6, which means it has 6 protons in its nucleus. Oxygen (äk'-si-jən) has an atomic number of 8, which means it has 8 protons in its nucleus.

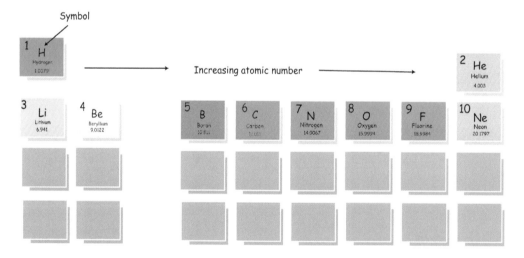

All of the elements have a symbol. For example, hydrogen (hī'-drə-jən) has the symbol "H," and carbon has the symbol "C." Notice that for these elements the symbol is the same as the first letter of the name. This is true for many elements because they have English names, like oxygen which has the symbol "O." But some names come from other languages. The name for sodium (sō'-dē-əm) comes from the Latin word *natrium,* so it has the symbol "Na." Tungsten comes from the German word *wolfram,* so it has the symbol "W." Other examples include gold, which has the symbol "Au" from the Latin word *aurum,* and lead (led), which has the symbol "Pb" from the Latin word *plumbum.*

As we just saw, the atomic number tells how many protons the atom contains. In an atom, the number of protons equals the number of electrons, so this number is also the number of electrons in an atom. For example, the smallest element is hydrogen. It has an atomic number of 1, which means it has only one proton. It also has only one electron, since *the number of protons equals the number of electrons.*

Atomic number

1

H

Hydrogen
1.0079

Symbol   Name

Atomic weight

Hydrogen has only one proton and no neutrons.

Though atoms are very small, each one has a weight called the atomic weight. For most atoms the atomic weight is very close to the sum of the protons and neutrons in the nucleus. Both protons and neutrons have an atomic weight of 1. Electrons are so small that they are given almost no weight at all. The number of neutrons for an atom can be calculated by subtracting the number of protons from the atomic weight.

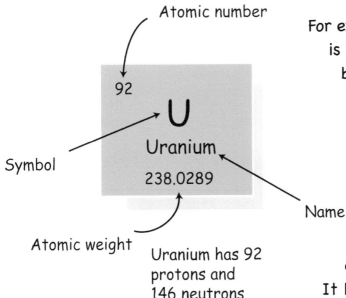

Atomic number

92

U

Uranium
238.0289

Symbol

Name

Atomic weight

Uranium has 92 protons and 146 neutrons

For example, the atomic weight of hydrogen is 1.0079, which is the number found below the name. To find the number of neutrons, the number of protons (1) is subtracted from the atomic weight (1.0079 or 1); 1 – 1 = 0. This means that hydrogen has no neutrons and only one proton in its nucleus.

The largest naturally occurring element is uranium (yü-rā′-nē-əm). It has an atomic number of 92, which means it has 92 protons and 92 electrons. It has an atomic weight of 238.0289. To calculate the number of neutrons, the number of protons is subtracted from the atomic weight (238 - 92 = 146), so uranium has 146 neutrons.

The elements in the periodic table are arranged vertically according to their chemical properties. All of the elements in a single column undergo similar chemical reactions and have similar chemical properties. All of the elements in the far right-hand column are called the noble gases. They are similar to each other because they don't react with other atoms or molecules. The elements in the far left-hand column are called the alkali (al'-kə-lī) metals. They are similar to each other because they react with lots of different atoms or molecules.

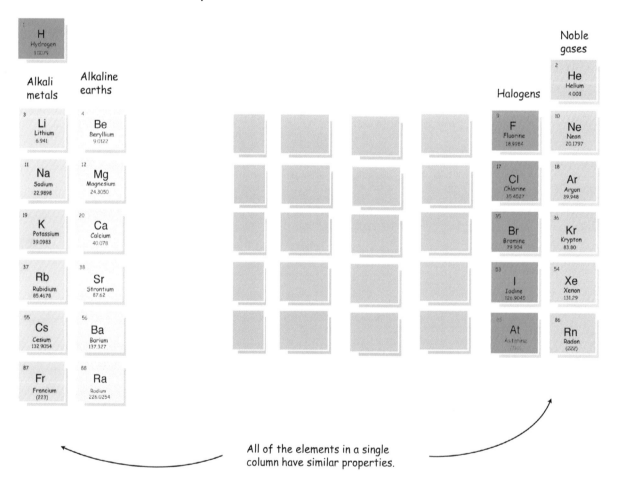

All of the elements in a single column have similar properties.

The periodic table of elements organizes a lot of information about the elements and their chemical properties. This table helps chemists predict the behavior of the elements and how they might interact with each other. Before all of the naturally occurring elements were known, Mendeleev used the organization of his table to predict many of the properties of the missing elements. The success of his predictions and the organization of his chart led to its acceptance as a major scientific accomplishment.

1.4 Summary

Here are the most important points to remember from this chapter:

○ All things, both living and nonliving, are made of atoms.

○ Atoms are made of protons, neutrons, and electrons.

○ In an atom, *the number of protons equals the number of electrons.*

○ All atoms (or elements) are found in the periodic table of elements.

○ The elements are arranged in the periodic table in groups that are similar.

Chapter 2 Molecules

2.1 From atoms to molecules

As we saw earlier, everything is made of atoms. Sometimes things are made of a single type of atom, like gold or silver, and sometimes things are made of more than one type of atom, like table salt, which is a combination of sodium and chlorine. When two or more atoms combine with each other, they make a molecule (mä'-li-kyül).

Recall that atoms are made of protons, neutrons, and electrons. Protons and neutrons are located in the center of an atom, and the electrons surround them. When two atoms come together, sometimes they will "stick" to each other. When this happens, a molecule is formed.

2.2 Forming bonds

How do atoms stick to each other to make molecules? As it turns out, *electrons* make atoms "stick" to each other. They do this by sharing the space inside their electron clouds.

For example, a single hydrogen atom has just one electron. When another hydrogen atom gets close enough, the two electron clouds combine, and the electrons from each of the two atoms share the combined space.

When this happens, the two atoms are said to form a bond. This simply means that the two atoms are now connected, or "stuck," to each other.

Two separate hydrogen atoms

+

One single hydrogen molecule

Space shared by both electrons

2.3 Types of bonds

There are two different kinds of bonds, and they differ only in how they share their electrons. Sometimes electrons are shared between the two atoms. This kind of bond is called a shared electron bond. Sometimes one atom takes more electrons for itself. This kind of bond is called an unshared electron bond. Molecules that have shared electron bonds behave very differently from molecules that have unshared electron bonds. This difference is quite important because it determines the way in which molecules interact with other molecules.

2.4 Shared electron bonds

A chlorine molecule (Cl_2) with shared electrons

The hydrogen molecule that we just saw is an example of a bond where the electrons are *equally* shared. Because the atoms are identical (they are both hydrogens), one atom cannot take more electrons for itself than the other atom does. This results in a bond with *shared* electrons, and in this particular case the electrons are equally shared. A bond with shared electrons is called a covalent (cō-vā'-lent) bond.

Bonds that are equally shared are *always* formed when two identical atoms, like two hydrogens, two oxygens, two nitrogens, or two chlorine atoms, combine to form a molecule.

However, covalent bonds also form between atoms that are *not* identical but still want to share electrons, like carbon and oxygen, carbon and hydrogen, and hydrogen and oxygen. The molecule formed by one carbon atom and four hydrogen atoms also has bonds with shared electrons, and these are covalent bonds.

A carbon atom and four hydrogens (CH_4) with shared electrons

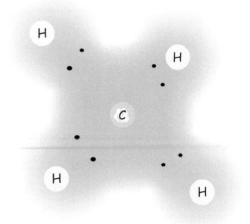

2.5 Unshared electron bonds

Sometimes the electrons are not shared between the two atoms. When this happens, one atom tends to want more electrons for itself and is not willing to share electrons with the other atom. This results in a bond with *unshared* electrons. This type of bond is called an ionic (ī-ä′-nik) bond.

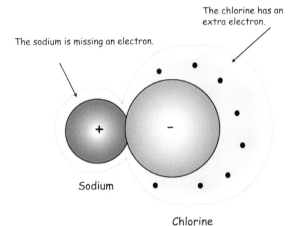

The sodium is missing an electron.

The chlorine has an extra electron.

Sodium

Chlorine

The electrons in the bond between a sodium atom and a chlorine atom are *not* shared. The sodium atom gives away one of its electrons to the chlorine atom. As a result, the sodium atom has fewer electrons than it would normally have if it were alone, and the chlorine atom has more electrons than it would normally have if it were alone.

The molecule formed by sodium and chlorine is called sodium (sō′-dē-əm) chloride (klôr′-īd). Sodium chloride is also known as "table salt."

We use table salt to flavor our food. The crystals that we sprinkle out are made of many, many molecules of sodium chloride packed together. The fact that the electrons are not shared in sodium chloride makes table salt very easy to dissolve in water (see Chapter 6), and this helps us taste it when we put it on our food.

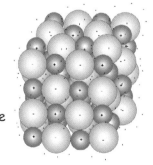

Sodium chloride crystal

2.6 Bonding rules

The number of electrons an atom has also determines *how many* bonds an atom can form. An atom cannot form just any number of bonds with another atom.

For example, a hydrogen atom has only one electron, so it usually forms only one bond. Carbon, on the other hand, has a total of 6 electrons. However, only 4 of those electrons are available to make bonds, so carbon atoms usually form a total of 4 bonds. Nitrogen (nī'-trə-jən) has only three available electrons and usually forms three bonds. Oxygen (äk'-si-jən), with two available electrons, typically forms only two bonds.

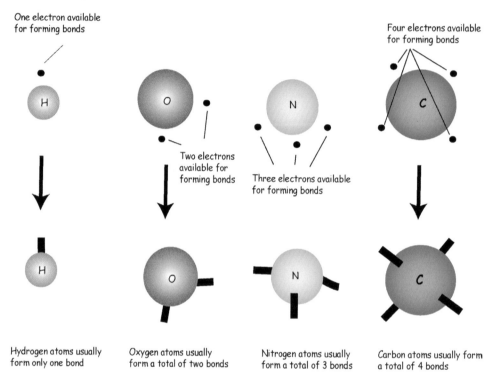

One electron available for forming bonds

Four electrons available for forming bonds

Two electrons available for forming bonds

Three electrons available for forming bonds

Hydrogen atoms usually form only one bond

Oxygen atoms usually form a total of two bonds

Nitrogen atoms usually form a total of 3 bonds

Carbon atoms usually form a total of 4 bonds

2.7 Shapes of molecules

Water molecules do not form these shapes.

Each type of molecule has its own particular shape. For example, when two hydrogen atoms bond with a single oxygen atom to make H_2O, or water, the molecules are bent. All water molecules are bent because of the way their electrons are arranged on the oxygen atom. This fact gives water special features that make it essential for all living things.

Bent water molecules

2.8 Summary

Here are the most important points to remember from this chapter:

○ When two or more atoms combine, they form a molecule.

○ Atoms in a molecule are "stuck" to each other with bonds.

○ Bonds are formed with the electrons from each atom in a molecule.

○ Shared electron bonds are called covalent bonds.

○ Unshared electron bonds are called ionic bonds.

○ The number of bonds an atom can form depends on the number of available electrons.

○ Different kinds of molecules have different shapes, but molecules of the same kind always have the same shape.

Chapter 3 Chemical Reactions

3.1 Introduction

What happens inside a battery? How does a car use gasoline to run? What happens to an egg when it's fried in a pan? All of these situations are examples of chemical reactions at work. Chemical reactions happen almost everywhere we look. They provide the energy that powers many things including cars, toys, plants, and animals. Our own bodies work by means of many complex chemical reactions.

A chemical reaction occurs whenever bonds between atoms and molecules are created or destroyed.

The following are four general types of chemical reactions:

1. Combination (käm-bə-nā'-shən) reactions occur when two or more molecules combine with each other to make a new molecule.

2. Decomposition (dē-käm-pə-zi'-shən) reactions occur when a molecule decomposes, or breaks apart, into two or more molecules.

3. Displacement (dis-plās'-mənt) reactions occur when one atom kicks another atom out of a molecule.

4. Exchange (eks-chānj') reactions occur when one atom trades places with another atom.

3.2 Combination reaction

In a combination reaction, two or more molecules combine to form a single product.

The reaction of sodium and chlorine (klôr'-ēn) to make sodium chloride, or table salt, is an example of a combination reaction. In this reaction two sodium atoms combine with one molecule of chlorine gas to make two molecules of sodium chloride.

Sodium + Chlorine

Sodium chloride
(Table salt)

3.3 Decomposition reaction

In a decomposition reaction, molecules of one type break apart or *decompose* to make two or more products. The breakup of water into hydrogen and oxygen gases is an example of a decomposition reaction.

Two water molecules (H_2O)

High heat or electric current

Oxygen gas

+

Hydrogen gas

3.4 Displacement reaction

A third general type of chemical reaction is the displacement reaction.

Sodium

Water

Sodium

Water

Sodium Hydroxide (NaOH)

Hydrogen gas (H_2)

Na O H

Sodium Hydroxide (NaOH)

In this reaction, one atom will remove another atom from a compound to form a new product.

The formation of sodium hydroxide from two water molecules and two sodium atoms is an example of a displacement reaction. For each of the two water molecules, one sodium atom (shown as a blue ball labeled "Na") kicks one hydrogen atom (shown as a gray ball labeled "H") out of the water molecule. Then the sodium atom combines with the remaining oxygen atom and hydrogen atom (called a hydroxide [hī-dräk'-sīd] ion) to make a new molecule called sodium hydroxide. Hydrogen gas is formed by the two hydrogen atoms that were kicked out of the two water molecules by the sodium atoms.

3.5 Exchange reaction

The fourth type of general chemical reaction is the exchange reaction. In this reaction, the atoms of one molecule trade places with the atoms of another molecule to form two new molecules.

The reaction of hydrochloric acid (HCl) and sodium hydroxide (NaOH) is an example of an exchange reaction. The hydrogen atom in the HCl molecule trades places with the sodium atom in the NaOH molecule to make two new molecules, sodium chloride (table salt) and water.

Cl

H

Hydrogen chloride

+

Na

O

H

Sodium hydroxide

O

H   H

H_2O
Water

Na   Cl

Sodium chloride
(table salt)

These are the basic types of simple chemical reactions. Some reactions that have many components are much more complicated than those outlined in this chapter, but most chemical reactions fall into one of these four categories.

3.6 Spontaneous or not?

Not all chemical reactions are spontaneous (spän-tā'-nē-əs). Spontaneous means the reaction happens all by itself, just by mixing the chemicals. The exchange reaction of hydrochloric acid (HCl) and sodium hydroxide (NaOH) is a spontaneous reaction; however, not all chemical reactions are spontaneous. The decomposition reaction of water into hydrogen gas and oxygen gas is *not* a spontaneous reaction. It requires either high heat or an electric current. It's a good thing that not all reactions occur spontaneously. Imagine how difficult it would be to swim or sail a boat or even get a drink, if water spontaneously decomposed into hydrogen gas and oxygen gas!

3.7 Evidences of chemical reactions

To determine whether or not a chemical reaction has occurred, chemists look for certain signs, or evidences, of a change.

There are several signs that tell scientists when a chemical reaction has occurred.

A chemist may look for bubbles being released when something gets added to something else. Bubbles indicate that a gas formed during the reaction.

Bubbles forming

Or, if two solutions are mixed, the resulting new solution might change color.

Color change

Sometimes when two solutions are mixed, a temperature change occurs, and the solution gets either hotter or colder.

Temperature change

Finally, another indication that a chemical reaction has taken place is the formation of a precipitate (pri-si′-pə-tāt), which can look like colored sand, mud, dust, or snow forming in a solution. A precipitate forms when the new molecules being made from the chemical reaction do not dissolve in the solution.

These are some of the ways that chemists can tell when a chemical reaction has taken place.

Precipitation

3.8 Summary

Here are the most important points to remember from this chapter:

○ A chemical reaction occurs whenever bonds between atoms and molecules are created or destroyed.

○ There are different kinds of chemical reactions. They are as follows:
> combination reactions where molecules join
> decomposition reactions where molecules break apart
> displacement reactions where atoms are removed from molecules
> exchange reactions where atoms of one molecule trade places with atoms of another molecule

○ Not all chemical reactions occur spontaneously.

○ Sometimes changes occur that indicate a chemical reaction has taken place. These changes include bubble formation, color changes, temperature changes, and the formation of precipitates (precipitation).

Chapter 4 Acids, Bases, and pH

4.1 Introduction

One very important type of chemical reaction is the acid-base reaction. Acid-base reactions are a very special kind of exchange reaction. Recall that in an exchange reaction, the atoms of one molecule trade places with the atoms of another molecule.

The chemical reaction of vinegar with baking soda is an acid-base reaction. Vinegar, or acetic acid, is an acid, and baking soda, or sodium bicarbonate, is a base. When vinegar and baking soda are mixed, one of the hydrogen atoms of the vinegar trades places with the sodium atom of the baking soda. This is a type of exchange reaction.

Acetic acid
(vinegar)
ACID

Sodium bicarbonate
(baking soda)
BASE

A hydrogen atom from the vinegar breaks away and replaces the sodium on the baking soda.

As we have already seen, when vinegar and baking soda are mixed together, bubbles are released. The bubbles are evidence that a chemical reaction has occurred.

4.2 The pH scale

Acids and bases have a special property that can be used to identify them. This property is called pH (pronounced "P" "H"). The pH is a measure of how acidic or how basic a solution is. The pH of pure water is 7. Pure water is neutral (nü'-trǝl), neither acidic nor basic. If a substance is an acid and it is added to pure water to form a mixture called a solution, the pH will be LOWER than 7. If a substance is a base, adding it to pure water will RAISE the pH of the solution above 7.

pH = 7: The solution is neither an acid nor a base—it is neutral.
pH less than 7: The solution is an acid.
pH more than 7: The solution is a base.

The next chart shows the pH of various solutions. Notice that the pH for blood is near 7, close to the pH of water. Our bodies are made mostly of water, and blood carries nutrients throughout our bodies. It is important that the pH of blood be near 7 since many of our cells and tissues would be damaged if the pH were much higher or much lower than 7. However, notice that the pH for stomach fluid is even lower than the pH for vinegar. Why is stomach fluid so acidic? As it turns out, your stomach makes hydrochloric (hī-drə-klôr'-ik) acid, HCl. This acid helps to begin breaking down your food so that it can be carried to other places in your body. Your stomach has a special lining on the inside that is designed to prevent the acidic stomach fluid from causing damage.

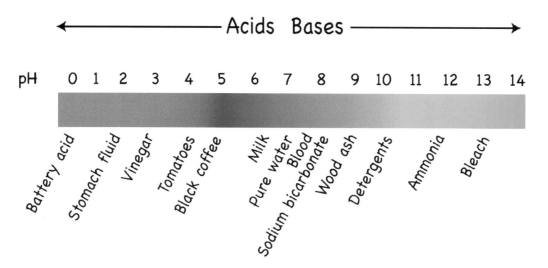

4.3 Properties of acids and bases

In the chart to the right, some general properties of acids and bases are shown. For example, vinegar, tomatoes, and black coffee are all acids, and all have a sour taste. It turns out that most acids are sour tasting. Grapefruit, for example, is not on the chart, but it is very sour. The juice inside a grapefruit contains a lot of citric (si'-trik) acid. Detergents and many cleaners feel slippery. This is because many cleaners are basic, and slipperiness tends to be a property of bases.

General Properties	
Acids	Bases
sour in taste	bitter in taste
not slippery to the touch	slippery to the touch
dissolve metals	react with metals to form precipitates

Some acids and bases are very poisonous or corrosive and can easily harm you. Battery acid, for example, can burn your skin if it happens to spill. It can also make you very sick if eaten.

4.4 Measuring pH

A better way to tell if something is an acid or a base is the pH. The pH of a solution can be measured in a variety of ways.

pH meter

Electrode

One way is to use a pH meter. A pH meter is an electronic device that measures the pH directly. A small stick, called an electrode (i-lek'-trōd), is placed into the solution, and the pH is read from the meter.

Another way to measure pH is to use pH paper, which is special paper that changes color when placed in either an acid or a base. Litmus paper is a very common type of pH paper. If blue litmus paper is placed in an acidic solution, the paper turns red. If red litmus paper is placed in a basic solution, the paper turns blue.

pH < 4.5
Acidic

pH > 8.3
Basic

Litmus paper

Litmus paper has special chemicals absorbed into the fiber of the paper. These chemicals are called acid-base indicators. The indicator that is in litmus paper is a natural dye that comes from lichens (lī'-kenz), a type of tree moss. Indicators are usually organic molecules (molecules made up of mostly carbon, hydrogen, and oxygen), and the color of these chemicals depends on the pH of the solution.

There are different kinds of acid-base indicators. Some indicators change colors at very low pH, and others don't change until the pH is very high. Some indicators even change colors twice. The next chart shows a few acid-base indicators and the pH range in which they change color.

From the above chart of acid-base indicators, we can see that crystal violet changes colors at very low pH. Below pH 1, crystal violet is yellow, but above pH 1 it is blue. Now look at phenolphthalein (fē-nəl-thā'-lēn). Below pH 9 phenolphthalein is not colored, but above pH 9 it turns pink. pH indicators are very useful for finding the pH of a solution and determining whether it is an acid or a base.

In general, any molecule that changes color when the pH changes can be considered an acid-base indicator. There are many different acid-base indicators.

4.5 Summary

Here are the most important points to remember from this chapter:

◦ Acids and bases react with each other in a special kind of exchange reaction.

◦ The pH tells whether a solution is an acid or a base.

◦ pH can be measured by pH meters, pH paper, and acid-base indicators.

Chapter 5 Acid–Base Neutralization

5.1 Introduction

When an acid is added to a base, or a base is added to an acid, a chemical reaction occurs. We saw this earlier with the reaction between vinegar (an acid) and baking soda (a base). Recall that an acid-base reaction is called an exchange reaction because the atoms in one molecule trade places with the atoms in the other molecule.

An acid-base reaction is also called a neutralization (nü-trə-li-zā'-shən) reaction. When an acid reacts with a base, the atoms that make the acid acidic (hydrogen ions) react with the atoms that make the base basic (hydroxide ions) to form water and a salt. When this happens, the acid and base neutralize (nü'-trə-līz) each other.

The reaction of acetic acid and sodium bicarbonate is actually a combination of two reactions. The initial step is the acid-base portion of the reaction, where the hydrogen ion of the acid trades places with the sodium ion of the base. The next step is a decomposition reaction, where carbon dioxide is produced and released as bubbles.

Acid-base exchange reaction

Acetic acid (Vinegar)

Sodium bicarbonate (Baking soda)

A hydrogen ion from the vinegar breaks away and replaces the sodium ion on the baking soda.

The vinegar picks up the free sodium ion and forms sodium acetate.

Sodium acetate

Decomposition reaction

hydroxyl ion

hydrogen ion

water

Carbon dioxide is released as a gas and bubbles away.

The pH of the solution is neutral (pH = 7) if equal amounts of acetic acid and sodium bicarbonate have been added.

The sodium acetate stays in the solution dissolved in the water.

When equal amounts of acid react with equal amounts of base, both the acid and the base are neutralized, and the solution becomes neutral—neither acidic nor basic. In the case of vinegar and baking soda, the acid was turned into a salt, and the baking soda was converted into carbon dioxide and water. The carbon dioxide went away as bubbles, and the salt and water stayed in the jar.

5.2 Concentration

The fact that equal amounts of acids and bases can neutralize each other is very useful for chemists. Sometimes chemists are very concerned with *how much* of something they have. More precisely, they want to know how many molecules they might have in a given volume of solution. You can see that if you have more acid molecules in one solution than in another, it will be more acidic.

The number of molecules in a given volume of solution is called the concentration (kän-sən-trā'-shən). If there are a lot of molecules in a solution, then it is concentrated. If there are fewer molecules, then the solution is dilute (dī-loot').

In the laboratory, concentrated (pure) acetic acid is called glacial (glā'-shəl) acetic (ə-sē'-tik) acid. It has a very strong odor, and bottles of it must be opened in a special place called a fume hood. It would badly burn you if spilled on your skin. However, dilute acetic acid is vinegar. It is the same acid, but much less concentrated; therefore, vinegar is OK (and delicious) to eat on a salad.

Concentrated
acetic acid

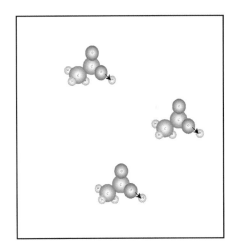

Dilute
acetic acid

Sometimes it may be necessary to neutralize an acid with a base or a base with an acid. For example, when someone eats too many chili cheese fries, he or she might suffer from acid indigestion. When a person has acid indigestion, the stomach has produced too much acid, and this excess acid causes pain. A good way to reduce that pain is to neutralize the acid. There are many different antacids that are used to neutralize stomach acid. All antacids are bases, and when someone uses an antacid, their stomach acid is neutralized. Antacids are not very strong or concentrated, so they are safe to eat when the need arises.

5.3 Titration

Remember that when the concentration of an acid equals the concentration of a base, the acid and base neutralize each other. The fact that equal amounts of acids and bases neutralize each other can be used to find the concentration of an *unknown* acid or base.

When an acid is slowly added to a base or a base added to an acid, the neutralization reaction can be observed in detail. This process is called a titration (tī-trā′-shən).

An acid, no base added.

One spoonful of base added but the solution is still acidic.

Two spoonfuls of base added. The solution is beginning to change color.

With three spoonfuls of base added, the acid has been neutralized. ⟶ If the concentration of the base is known, the concentration of the acid can be determined from this titration.

5.4 Plotting data

One way to examine the titration in detail is to plot or graph the data. A plot is a handy tool that scientists use to understand data. Plots can be made of almost any data. For example, you might notice that the older members in your family are usually taller than the younger members, so you could say that there is a connection between *age* and *height*. A plot can be made to illustrate the relationship between age and height. To make a plot of age vs. (versus) height, a line is drawn horizontally across the paper. Another line is drawn perpendicular to the first (vertically) and crosses over the first line on the left-hand side. These two lines are called axes (ak′-sēz); each one is called an axis (ak′-səs). To plot age vs. height, the bottom axis is labeled "age" and the vertical axis is labeled "height." Now, data can be collected, and it might look something like this:

Age	Height
age 1	2 ft
age 6	3 ft
age 8	4 ft
age 11	5 ft
age 30	5 1/2 ft
age 40	5 4/5 ft
age 60	5 3/4 ft

To plot the data in this example, the age of the person is marked on the graph with a vertical dotted line. Then, the height of the person is marked with a horizontal dotted line, and the point where the two lines intersect is marked with a red dot. A solid black line can be drawn to connect all of the red dots (points) on the plot. From the plot we can tell that, in general, as a person gets older, he or she grows taller. (The solid black line goes up as the age goes up.) The graph also shows that a person stops growing when he or she reaches a certain age. (The solid black line levels off, showing that no significant growth occurs after age 20 or so.) Plotting is a tool that scientists use to organize their data so that it is easier to understand.

Height in feet (vertical axis, values 1–10)

Age in years (horizontal axis, values 0, 1, 6, 8, 10, 20, 30, 40, 50, 60)

5.5 Plot of an acid-base titration

A plot of an acid-base titration has a horizontal axis labeled "Amount of base (or acid) added," and a vertical axis labeled "pH" or "color." A titration of a base into an acid may look something like this:

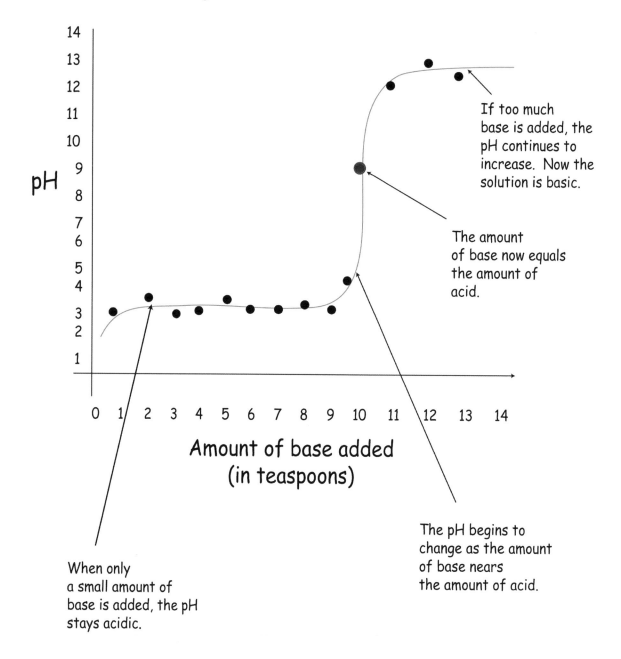

If too much base is added, the pH continues to increase. Now the solution is basic.

The amount of base now equals the amount of acid.

pH

Amount of base added
(in teaspoons)

When only a small amount of base is added, the pH stays acidic.

The pH begins to change as the amount of base nears the amount of acid.

By doing a titration, the chemist can determine the concentration of an unknown acid or base.

5.6 Summary

Here are the most important points to remember from this chapter:

◦ An acid and a base neutralize each other in an acid-base reaction.

◦ Equal amounts of acid and base completely neutralize each other.

◦ The concentration of an unknown acid or base can be found using a titration.

Chapter 6 Mixtures

6.1 Introduction

Sometimes things that look like they are made up of only one item are really made of many items. For example, when we eat cake we may think that we are eating only cake, but cake has many different ingredients in it. It has flour, eggs, butter, maybe some salt, water or milk, baking powder and, hopefully, chocolate.

Cake is really a mixture of many ingredients:

Fats

Eggs

Proteins

Water

Some of the ingredients themselves are also mixtures, so a cake is a mixture of mixtures!

Starch

Sugar

Candy sprinkles

6.2 Types of mixtures

There are two main types of mixtures called homogeneous (hō-mə-jē'-nē-əs) and heterogeneous (he-tə-rə-jē'-nē-əs) mixtures.

The salt is the same everywhere.

Salt water is a homogeneous mixture.

Homo comes from the Greek word *homos* which means "the same," and geneous comes from the Greek word *genos* which means "kind," so a homogeneous mixture is a mixture of "the same kind." An example of a homogeneous mixture is salt water. In a glass of salt water, the salt water is the same everywhere in the glass. The top of the glass does not have different salt water than the bottom of the glass does, so salt water is considered a *homogeneous mixture.*

More ice cubes at the top than at the bottom.

Ice water is a heterogeneous mixture.

Hetero comes from the Greek word *heteros* which means "other," so a heterogeneous mixture is a mixture of "other kind." An example of a heterogeneous mixture is ice water. Although ice and water are both water, ice has different properties than water. Ice floats in water. In a glass of ice water there will be more ice at the top of the glass than at the bottom of the glass. The mixture of ice and water is not the same throughout, so it is called a *heterogeneous mixture.*

6.3 Like dissolves like

Homogeneous mixtures are made of substances that like to mix. When salt is added to water, the water molecules break the salt crystals apart into sodium ions and chloride ions. The salt is said to dissolve or "break apart" in the water. When this happens, a homogeneous saltwater mixture is created.

Sodium chloride crystal being dissolved by water molecules.

Water molecules

Sodium chloride dissolved in water to make a homogeneous mixture of sodium ions, chloride ions, and water molecules.

Two substances that do not like to mix make heterogeneous mixtures. For example, when oil is added to water, the oil stays in little droplets or floats to the top. No matter how hard these two are shaken, they simply do not mix.

Why does salt dissolve in water but not in oil? As it turns out, the properties of the individual molecules determine if something will dissolve or not. The rule is:

Like dissolves like.

This means that molecules that are like each other will dissolve in each other, and molecules that are not alike will not dissolve in each other.

Salt and water are alike in some ways, and oil and water are not.

Water molecules and salt molecules are alike in that they both have charged parts. Recall that the bond for a sodium chloride molecule is an ionic (unshared) bond. Ionic bonds are easy to pull apart. When this happens, the chlorine and the sodium become ions and are charged. (An ion is an atom that has gained or lost an electron.) Water molecules can easily pull the sodium and chloride bonds apart because water is positively charged on one end and negatively charged on the other end.

The bonds holding the water molecules together do not break apart because the bonds in a water molecule are not ionic bonds but are covalent bonds (see Chapter 2). Instead, the charged ends of the water molecules surround the free sodium ions and the free chloride ions.

Positively charged

Negatively charged

Charged ends of water molecules surrounding the charged ions

Note that the negative ends of the water molecules surround the positive sodium ions, and the positive ends of the water molecules surround the negative chloride ions. Since the water molecules and the salt molecules are both charged and are thus "alike" in certain chemical ways, one will *dissolve* in the other.

Oil molecules, on the other hand, are not charged. Oil molecules are long chains of hydrogen and carbon atoms hooked together, and they do not carry any effective charge.

The molecule that makes up vegetable oil, glycerol trioleate (gli'-sə-rôl trī-ō'-lē-āt), is made of three long chains of carbons and hydrogens connected together on one end. This molecule has no charged parts; therefore, it is not *like* water and cannot mix with or dissolve in water. However, it can be dissolved in other molecules that are also not charged, like mineral oil (octadecane) or even gasoline!

Glycerol trioleate
(vegetable oil)

Octadecane
(mineral oil)

The principle that like dissolves like can be used to decide how something might be cleaned. For example, those things that dissolve in water, like ammonia, bleach, and water-based paints, can be cleaned with water; however, those things that do not dissolve in water, like grease and oil-based paints, cannot be cleaned with water. Many cleaning fluids, like mineral spirits, are made of molecules that are not charged and can, therefore, dissolve oil-based paints or grease.

6.4 Soap

Mineral spirits and gasoline, although effective on grease, are not very useful for washing olive oil from your hands after preparing salad. Also, these solutions are very poisonous and can easily catch on fire. So what can be used instead?

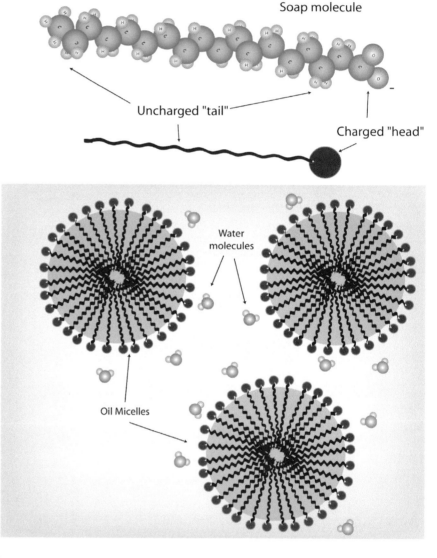

Soap, of course! Soaps are molecules that have both a charged end *and* an uncharged end. These molecules are able to dissolve oil in water because they have an *uncharged* part (that likes oil) and a *charged* part (that likes water).

When soap comes into contact with an oil molecule, the uncharged part (or oily part) mixes with the oil. The charged part of the soap molecule does not want to mix with the oil, so it stays mixed with the water. This results in the formation of very tiny droplets called micelles (mī-celz'). On the inside of a micelle, the greasy, uncharged end of the soap is dissolved in the oil, and on the outside of a micelle, the charged end is dissolved in the water. These tiny droplets can then be washed away with water.

6.5 Summary

Here are the most important points to remember from this chapter:

○ There are two types of mixtures: homogeneous and heterogeneous.

○ Homogeneous mixtures are made by things that are "like" each other.

○ Heterogeneous mixtures are made by things that are "not like" each other.

○ Things that are "alike" dissolve in each other: *Like dissolves like.*

○ Soap helps oil "dissolve" in water.

Chapter 7 Separating Mixtures

7.1 Introduction

Sometimes mixtures are desirable and result in tasty cakes, refreshing Kool-Aid, and clean hands, but other times mixtures need to be separated. For example, when boiling spaghetti noodles, the mixture of spaghetti and hot water first needs to be separated before sauce can be added. To do this, the

spaghetti is placed in a sieve or colander. The water runs through the small holes of the sieve, but the spaghetti is retained because it is too large. This is a simple example of separation. Separation is the process of removing one or more items from a mixture.

7.2 Filtration

Separating spaghetti noodles from water is called filtration (fil-trā'-shən). Filtration can be used to separate two or more things of different sizes. Since the spaghetti noodles are much larger than the water molecules, it is easy to separate them with a sieve. A sieve is a kind of filter. The holes in a filter are called pores. The size of the pores in a filter determines the size of things that can be separated. Large pores, like in the sieve, separate large things, like spaghetti, from smaller things like water. Filters with small pores can separate small molecules from large molecules.

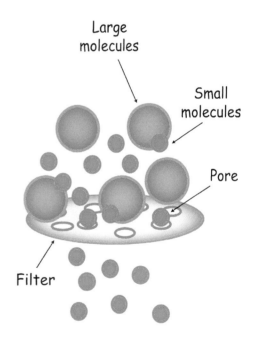

The smaller the pore size, the smaller the molecule that can be separated.

7.3 Evaporation

Filtration cannot be used to separate items of the same size. For example, spaghetti noodles cannot be separated from linguine noodles with a sieve since they are nearly the same size. Likewise, salt molecules cannot be separated from water molecules by filtration since they also are nearly the same size.

So just how does one separate salt molecules from water molecules? One way is by using a different technique called evaporation (i-va-pə-rā'-shən). When water is allowed to evaporate, the salt gets left behind as a solid.

7.4 Solids, liquids, and gases

Many molecules, like water, exist in three different *states*. These states are the solid state (for example, ice), the liquid state (liquid water), and the gaseous state (steam). We know that if an ice cube is placed into a hot pan it begins to melt and eventually disappears. What happened? Did the water vanish and cease to be water? No, the water simply changed from the solid state (ice) to the liquid state (water) to the gaseous state (water vapor). It *disappears* because our eyes cannot see the tiny water molecules when they are a gas.

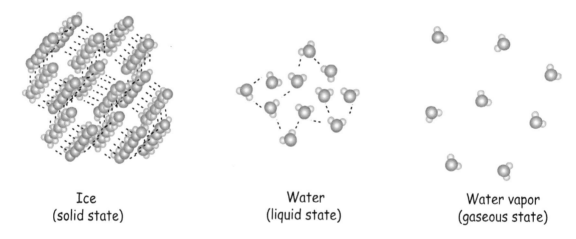

Ice
(solid state)

Water
(liquid state)

Water vapor
(gaseous state)

Water molecules like to "stick" to each other. This causes the molecules to form ice and liquid water. When heat is applied, the ice cube melts because the heat is adding "energy" to the molecules. This energy causes the molecules to move faster and faster. Soon the molecules are moving so fast they cannot stick to each other very well. Eventually the molecules have enough energy to completely break away from each other and become a gas.

Even without added heat, water molecules can still turn into a gas, but they do it more slowly. This is called evaporation. To separate water from salt molecules by evaporation, the water slowly turns into a gas and floats away. We say that the water has evaporated, leaving the salt molecules behind.

7.5 Chromatography

What if the molecules can't be separated by evaporation?

Another technique used to separate mixtures is chromatography (krō-mə-tä'-grə-fē). Chromatography relies on the fact that different molecules stick to each other in different ways. Chromato comes from the Greek word *chroma*, which means "color," and graphy comes from the Greek word *graphe,* which means "to write," so chromatography means "to write with color." This technique is so named because chromatography was originally used to separate colored compounds. Today, however, chromatography is used to separate substances of all kinds.

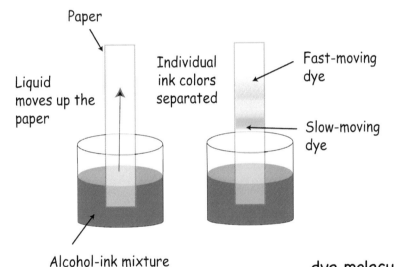

Paper

Individual ink colors separated

Liquid moves up the paper

Fast-moving dye

Slow-moving dye

Alcohol-ink mixture

The simplest form of chromatography can be carried out easily by standing a strip of paper in a solution. This is called paper chromatography. Because different molecules stick to paper in different ways, the molecules can be separated. For example, ink is usually a mixture of several dye molecules of different colors. The individual colors in ink can be separated from each other by using paper chromatography. To do this, the ink is dissolved in alcohol, or some other solvent (säl'-vənt), and one end of a thin strip of paper is dipped into the ink-alcohol mixture. The alcohol will begin to creep up the paper and carry the dye molecules with it. The different colors in the ink stick to the paper differently, so they move up at different rates. Soon, all of the colors in the ink are separated.

There are other kinds of chromatography, like gas chromatography where different gas molecules are separated from each other; however, all types of chromatography operate on similar principles.

7.6 Summary

Here are the most important points to remember from this chapter:

° Mixtures can be separated using different methods including filtration, evaporation, and chromatography.

° Filtration is used to separate smaller things from larger things.

° Evaporation can be used to separate molecules that evaporate from molecules that don't evaporate.

° Paper chromatography can be used to separate different colors in ink.

° There are three states of matter: solids, liquids, and gases. The molecules in a solid are closer together than the molecules in a liquid. In a gas, the molecules are far apart from each other.

Chapter 8   Energy Molecules

8.1 Introduction

Have you ever wondered why we need to eat food? We may know from experience that when we skip a meal or are unable to eat because of illness, we become weak and lack energy. Our bodies require food to help us grow and keep our "engines running." Without food we would not survive.

Unlike plants, we cannot stick our feet in the soil, lift our hands to the sun, and make our own food. In fact, we rely on plants and animals to provide the food our bodies need to keep us going. But what is in food and what does it do for us?

8.2 Nutrients

There are many different kinds of nutrients our bodies require to stay healthy. These include vitamins, proteins (prō'-tēnz), fats, and carbohydrates (kär-bō-hī'-drāts). We get these important nutrients from eating a variety of foods. The nutrients we get from eating foods provide the necessary molecules our bodies need to grow and function properly. Vitamins, like those found in carrots, help our eyes to work. Fats found in vegetable oil and butter help our brains and other tissues to function. Proteins from fish and meats help our bones to heal and our muscles to grow. Carbohydrates, like those found in bread, potatoes, and sweets, provide us with "energy."

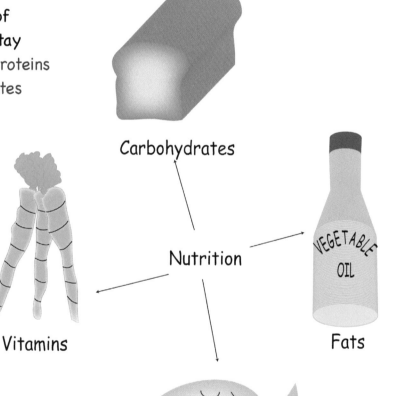

Carbohydrates

Vitamins

Nutrition

Fats

Proteins

8.3 Carbohydrates

What are carbohydrates and how do they provide energy for our bodies? The name "carbohydrate" is a general term for many different kinds of molecules that contain carbon, oxygen, and hydrogen. *Carbo* means "carbon" and *hydrate* means "water," so carbohydrate means "a combination of carbon and water."

Glucose
a simple sugar

The simplest carbohydrates are the sugars. Sugars are relatively small molecules. They taste sweet and can be easily broken down by our bodies to provide quick energy. The very simplest sugars are called monosaccharides (mä-nō-sa'-kə-rīdz). *Mono* comes from the Greek language and means "single," and saccharide (sa'-kə-rīd) means "sugar," so a monosaccharide is a "single sugar." The single sugars glucose and fructose are monosaccharides.

Fructose
a simple sugar

Sucrose
Glucose + Fructose

Sugar

Sucrose is an example of a disaccharide, which is a molecule made of two single sugars. Sucrose contains a molecule of glucose (glü'-kōs) that is hooked by a chemical bond to a single molecule of fructose (frük'-tōs). Sucrose is common table sugar, the same sugar that we buy in the store and put on strawberries. When a few monosaccharides are put together, they are called oligosaccharides (ä-li-gō-sa'-kə-rīdz). *Oligo* is Greek for "few," so an oligosaccharide is a "few sugars."

8.4 Starches

When more than a few saccharides, or sugars, are hooked together, the molecule is called a polysaccharide (pä-lē-sa'-kə-rīd). *Poly* means "many" so a polysaccharide has "many sugars." Polysaccharide molecules usually contain ten or more monosaccharides.

There are two general types of polysaccharides: starch and cellulose (sel'-yə-lōs). Starches are the molecules that provide our bodies with most of the energy we need in order to live and work. Potatoes, pasta, and bread are excellent sources starches.

There are three main kinds of starches. Glycogen (glī'-kə-jen) is a starch that animals produce in their livers and store in their muscles. Amylose (a'-mə-lōs) and amylopectin (a-mə-lō-pek'-tən) are two starches that are made by plants and are the main energy storage molecules found in rice and potatoes.

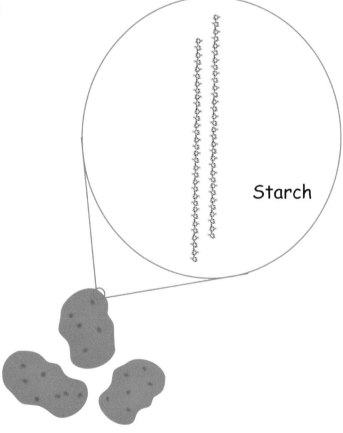

Starch

Potatoes

All of these polysaccharides are composed entirely of glucose molecules linked together to make long chains. They can have as many as 3,000 glucose units hooked together in a row.

So how do our bodies use these long chains of glucose for energy? We have special proteins in our bodies that break the long chains up into individual glucose molecules. The single glucose molecules are used directly by our bodies for energy, so if it is only the glucose our bodies need, why not eat only the simple sugars and have a diet rich in candy-coated sugar bomb cereals?

If we ate only simple sugars, our bodies would use up all of the energy in these molecules too quickly, and we would get tired. The long chains in the polysaccharides provide "storage" for the energy molecules so that we will have enough energy to ride bikes, swim, or run.

8.5 Cellulose

Cellulose differs from the starches only in how the glucose molecules are hooked together. The links between the glucose molecules in cellulose are different from the links between those of the starches. For the starches, the oxygen atom that connects the two glucose molecules is pointing "down." However, the oxygen between the two glucose molecules in cellulose is pointing "up." The direction of this bond is the only difference between these two molecules, but it makes a huge difference to us.

Starches

Links between glucoses

Cellulose

Cellulose is the main ingredient of wood, cotton, flax, wood pulp, and other plant fibers. It is even in grass. However, wood and grass are not main staples of our diet and are not served for Sunday brunch. In fact, although cellulose has the same glucose molecules that the starches have, humans cannot use cellulose for food energy at all.

Many animals, including humans, do not have the enzyme [en'-zīm] (protein) required to break the bonds between the glucose molecules in cellulose. Our enzymes only recognize the bonds in the starches, so we cannot graze the lawn for breakfast. Some animals, like cattle and horses, have bacteria that provide the necessary enzymes to break cellulose links, so these animals can eat grass for food energy, but we cannot.

8.6 Summary

Here are the most important points to remember from this chapter:

° Carbohydrates are molecules that give our bodies energy.

° Simple carbohydrates are sugars, and larger carbohydrates are starches and cellulose.

° Our bodies cannot use cellulose for energy because we cannot break the bonds in a cellulose molecule. Animals, such as horses and cows, can eat grass for food because they have bacteria that provide the enzymes needed to break the bonds in cellulose molecules.

Chapter 9 Polymers

9.1 Introduction

In the last chapter we saw that energy molecules are very long chains of single sugars. Polysaccharides are one kind of molecule in a class of molecules called polymers (pä'-lə-mərz). Recall that *poly* means "many." Mer comes from the Greek word *meros* which means "a part" or "unit," so a polymer is "many parts or units." Simply put, polymers are long-chain molecules made up of many smaller, repeating units.

Polymers, both natural and synthetic, play a critical role in our everyday lives. Everywhere we look, we are likely to run into polymers.

Plastic, cloth, and rubber are all polymers. This means that football helmets, car tires, hula hoops, yo-yos, volleyball nets, and volleyballs are all made of polymers.

9.2 Polymer uses

Polymers are used for pipes that bring clean water into our homes. Polymers are used for clothing and packaging, in hospitals and under the ocean. Polymers are indispensable in the modern world. Also, the most important molecules in our bodies are polymers, as we will see in the next chapter.

Some polymers are soft, and some are very hard. Some polymers are stretchable, and some are very stiff. What makes polymers so different? How can they have so many uses and so many different properties if they are only strings of small molecules?

9.3 Structure of polymers

Polymers are so different from each other because there are so many different ways to make polymers. A polymer is just a chain of smaller molecules called monomers (mä'-nə-mərz). Recall that *mono* means "one," so a monomer is "one unit." Polymers can be made entirely of one kind of monomer unit, like the starches and cellulose are, or they can be made of different monomer units, as in proteins and DNA (see next chapter). There are lots of different kinds of molecules that will form polymers.

For example, one common polymer that most plastics are made of is called polyethylene (pä-lē-e'-thə-lēn). Polyethylene chains are very simple chemically, just carbons and hydrogens. Polymers can be single chains, or they can have branches or side chains. They can be tightly packed, or they can be loosely packed. These differences give them some of their different properties.

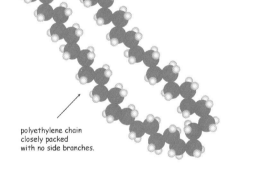

polyethylene chain with
loosely packed
side branches.

polyethylene chain
closely packed
with no side branches.

When the monomers for polyethylene are closely packed, the plastic is very hard. This plastic is used to make bottle caps, toys, sewer pipes, and the casing around electronic equipment such as TVs and radios. However, when polyethylene molecules are loosely packed, the plastic is much softer. This softer form of polyethylene is used to make plastic bags, squeeze bottles, plastic wrap for food, and other items. Both types of plastic have exactly the same kinds of molecules, but they differ in the way they are packed together.

9.4 Modifying polymers

In addition, polymer properties can change if single polymer molecules are connected to other single polymer molecules.

Polymer molecules
sliding past one another

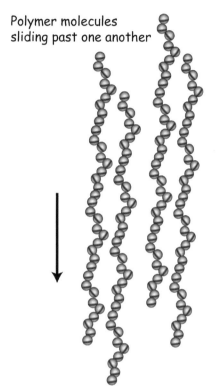

Natural rubber

For example, natural rubber is very soft and sticky when it is hot. It is not very useful for making tires and kitchen gloves because it is too soft and sticky. However, if natural rubber is heated with sulfur, it becomes harder and not sticky. This process is called vulcanization (vul-kə-ni-zā'-shən).

How does this work? The polymers in natural rubber are single chains and can easily slip past one another. This makes the rubber soft and sticky.

When natural rubber is heated to high temperatures with sulfur, the individual polymers become hooked together by sulfur bonds. This makes the rubber harder and easier to mold into things like tires or kitchen gloves.

Vulcanization is a way of making crosslinks between individual polymer chains. These crosslinks change the properties of the rubber.

Polymer molecules cannot slide past each other because of sulfur bonds

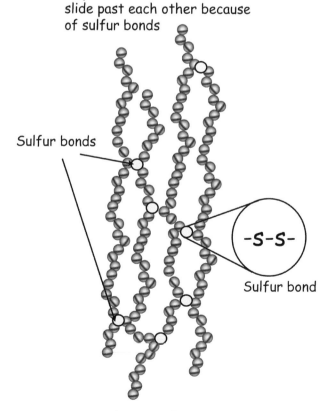

Sulfur bonds

-S-S-

Sulfur bond

Vulcanized rubber

9.5 Summary

Here are the most important points to remember from this chapter:

○ Polymers are long chains made of many repeating units. Carbohydrates (starches and cellulose) are a kind of polymer. Plastics are also made of polymers.

○ Polymers can have different shapes. They can be long chains, or they may have side branches. The different shapes give polymers different properties, like whether they are hard or soft.

○ Polymers can be modified, or changed, with chemicals or heat. The vulcanization of natural rubber to make it harder is an example of modifying a polymer.

Chapter 10   Biological Polymers, Proteins and DNA

10.1 Introduction

There are two very important polymers that all living things contain: proteins (prō'-tēnz) and DNA (say "D" "N" "A"). Proteins and DNA are biological polymers because they are found in biological organisms. Without proteins and DNA, life as we know it would not be possible.

10.2 Proteins

Amino acid

Proteins are polymers of amino (ə-mē'-nō) acids. An amino acid is a carbon atom with a carboxylic (kär-bäk-si'-lik) acid group and an amine (ə'-mēn) group attached. A carboxylic acid group is simply a carbon atom with two oxygens and one hydrogen attached. An amine group is a nitrogen atom with two hydrogens. Both of these groups are attached to a central carbon atom, which is called the "α"(alpha [al'-fə]) carbon.

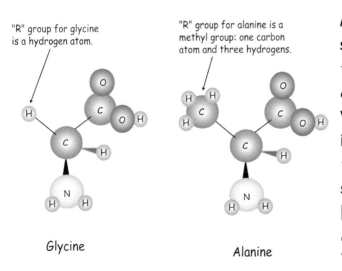

Glycine   Alanine

All amino acids have this basic structure, but not all amino acids are the same. There are 20 different amino acids commonly found in proteins. What makes each amino acid different is the "R" group that is attached to the α-carbon. The "R" group can be a single atom like hydrogen (as in glycine [glī'-sēn]), or it can be a collection of atoms as in alanine (al'-ə-nēn). The "R" group is different for each amino acid and gives each amino acid its own special properties.

10.3 Proteins are amino acid polymers

To form a protein, amino acids are hooked to each other through a particular type of bond. The bond between two amino acids is called a peptide (pep'-tīd) bond. A peptide bond occurs only between the amine group on one amino acid and the carbonyl group (a carbon atom double bonded to an oxygen atom) on the other amino acid. The "R" group is not involved in the bond.

Each amino acid in a protein is called a peptide unit. When fewer than 50 amino acids are hooked together, the molecule is usually called a polypeptide (pä-lē-pep'-tīd).

Peptides

Alanine

Glycine

Glycine

Peptide bonds

Three peptides connected together through peptide bonds.

However, when more than about 50 amino acids are connected, the molecule is called a protein.

10.4 Protein polymers form special shapes

Proteins don't remain as stretched out chains. They fold into different shapes. Because protein molecules are made with many different amino acids, they have many different shapes. Some form coils, others fold into balls, and some combine with other proteins to form even more complicated shapes.

stretched out protein

folds into a ball   OR   folds into a coil

Ball forms a "head"   Coil forms a "tail"

Kinesin head and tail

For example, the protein kinesin (ki-nē'-sin) has a head shaped like a ball and a tail made out of a long coil. Why are shapes important? Because...

the shape (structure) of a protein controls what it does.

Kinesin "walks" along a molecular "road" inside our cells. Kinesin is a protein that moves things around inside your cells. It acts like a little delivery truck that carries new parts from the places where they are made to the places they are needed in the cell. A full kinesin has two heads (that work like feet) and two tails wound together. It moves along a molecular road called a microtubule (mī-krō-tü'-byül) to deliver the cargo.

Kinesin "walks" along a molecular "road" and carries cargo

Kinesin protein
with two "feet"

Molecular "road" (microtubule)

10.5 Protein machines

Because they fold into many different shapes, proteins can act like tiny *machines*. They can do an amazing number of things. For example, some proteins, like kinesin, move molecules by "walking." Some are "pumps," some "read," some "cut," some "repair cuts," and others "build" or "assemble." These tiny machines do all of the work inside a cell!

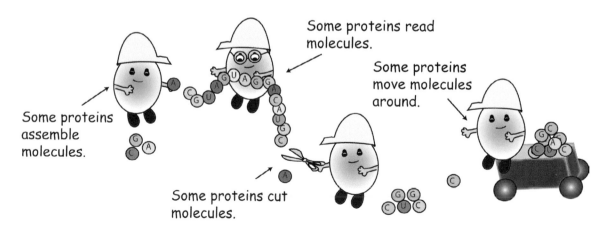

Some proteins read
molecules.

Some proteins
move molecules
around.

Some proteins
assemble
molecules.

Some proteins cut
molecules.

Proteins do all the work!

Kinesin is one such protein machine. Another is amylase (a'-mə-lās). Recall that in Chapter 8 we learned about starches, which are long chains of sugar molecules. Amylase is a "cutting" machine that cuts the long chain of amylose (a starch) to separate the individual sugar molecules contained in it. Our bodies can then use these sugar molecules for energy.

We digest most of our food in our stomach, but amylase is actually found in our mouth. It is in our saliva. When we eat food, the amylase begins to digest, or break down, amylose molecules in our mouth before we even swallow.

Sugar molecules

Amylase protein
(an amylose cutting machine)

Amylose

Amylase is a protein that breaks down amylose molecules into individual sugar molecules.

10.6 DNA

One of the molecules that proteins "read" and "cut" is DNA. DNA is an abbreviation that stands for deoxyribonucleic (dē-ăk′-sē-rī-bō-nü-klē′-ik) acid. Deoxyribonucleic acid (DNA) is a polymer that is made of nucleotides (nü′-klē-ə-tīdz), which are made of two parts: nucleic (nü-klä′-ik) acid bases and ribose (rī′-bōs) sugars. The bases are connected to the sugars, and the sugars are connected to each other.

Adenosine monophosphate (AMP)

A

Guanosine monophosphate (GMP)

G

Cytosine monophosphate (CMP)

C

Thymidine monophosphate (TMP)

T

There are four nucleic acid bases that are used to make the DNA polymer. They are called adenine (a′-də-nēn), guanine (gwä′-nēn), cytosine (sī′-tə-sēn), and thymine (thī′-mēn). They are given the single symbols A, G, C, and T.

10.7 DNA structure

DNA is a very unique polymer. It is actually two strands of polymers wrapped around each other like a twisted ladder. The bases in the middle of the ladder interact with each other, and the ribose sugars form the sides of the ladder. This twisted shape is called a double helix.

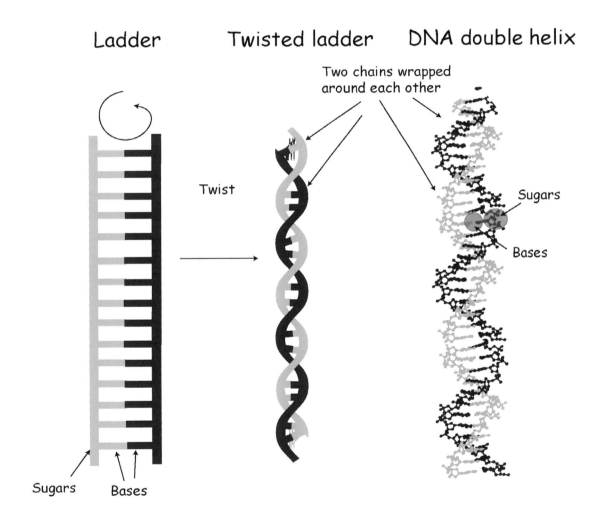

The bases (letters A, G, C, and T) along the DNA make up the genetic (jə-ne'-tik) code. The letters of DNA can be read by protein "reading machines," just like we read a book. DNA is the "library" for our cells, and the letters (bases) store all of the information cells need to run and make new cells.

10.8 Protein machines on DNA

DNA polymerase (pə-lim'-ə-rās) is a "DNA copy machine" that makes new copies of the DNA library. It is called a polymerase because it makes a DNA polymer. The polymerase "holds" the DNA, much as one might hold a rope. It crawls along the DNA, adding new nucleotides as it goes.

DNA polymerase on DNA

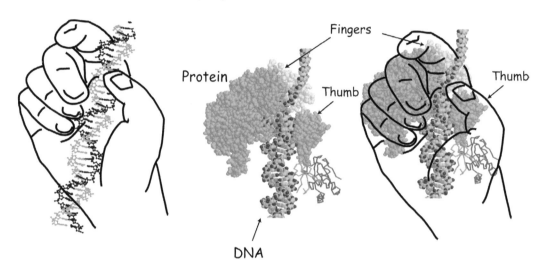

There are many kinds of polymerases that assemble other types of nucleic acid polymers, but all have the same basic structure because they all need to accomplish the same task. Again, the structure of a protein is partly determined by the task it needs to perform.

10.9 Summary

Here are the most important points to remember from this chapter:

° Proteins and DNA are polymers inside our bodies.

° Proteins do all of the work inside cells, including moving molecules, making molecules, and cutting and assembling molecules.

° DNA carries the genetic code, which tells cells how to grow.

Glossary-Index

cellulose (sel'-yə-lōs) ⊙ the polysaccharide that is the main structural molecule in plants, 48, 49.

charged ⊙ a molecule that has a positive or negative electric charge, 36.

chemical elements ⊙ the atoms that make up living and non-living things, 4.

chemical properties ⊙ the internal structures of elements that become evident during chemical reactions, 6.

chemical reaction ⊙ occurs when bonds between atoms and molecules are created or destroyed, 15-18.

chemistry ⊙ the field of science that studies the composition, structure and properties of matter, 2.

chlorine (klôr'-ēn) ⊙ the 17th element in the periodic table with the symbol Cl; has 17 protons, 17 electrons, and 18 neutrons; is a halogen and combines with sodium to make sodium chloride (table salt), 15.

chromatography (krō-mə-tä'-grə-fē) ⊙ [chroma, color, Gr.; graphe, to write, Gr.] a method for separating mixtures by passing a solution over a solid film or powder, 43.

citric (si'-trik) acid ⊙ an acid found in various fruits including grapefruit and oranges, 22.

combination (käm-bə-nā'-shən) reaction ⊙ a type of chemical reaction in which two or more molecules combine with each other to make a new molecule, 15.

concentrated (kän-sən-trā'-təd) solution ⊙ a solution containing many molecules of the dissolved substance in a given volume, 27.

concentration (kän-sən-trā'-shən) ⊙ the number of molecules in a given volume of solution, 27, 28.

covalent (cō-vā'-lent) bond ⊙ the attachment formed when two atoms are joined together and *share* their electrons, 10, 36.

crosslinks ⊙ the links between two long-chain polymer molecules, 54.

crystal violet ⊙ an acid-base indicator, 24.

cytosine (sī'-tə-sēn) [C] ⊙ one of the four nucleic acid bases that make DNA, 62, 63.

DNA [deoxyribonucleic acid (dē-äk'-sē-rī'-bō-nü-klē'-ik a'-səd)] ⊙ a polymer made of ribose sugars and the four nucleic acid bases (A, T, G, and C) that carry the genetic code, 57, 62-64.

DNA polymerase (pə-lim'-ə-rās) ⊙ the protein inside a cell that copies DNA, 64.

decomposition (dē-käm-pə-zi'-shən) reaction ⊙ a type of chemical reaction in which a molecule breaks apart into two or more molecules, 15, 16.

deoxyribonucleic acid ⊙ (see DNA)

dilute (dī-loot') ⊙ a solution containing few molecules of the dissolved substance per unit volume, 27.

disaccharide (dī-sa'-kə-rīd) ⊙ [Gr., *di,* two; Gr., *saccharide,* sugar] a molecule made of two single sugars, 47.

displacement (dis-plās'-mənt) reaction ⊙ a type of chemical reaction in which one atom takes the place of another atom to form new molecules, 15, 16.

dissolve ⊙ when the molecules in a solid that is mixed into a liquid like water break apart from each other and become loose in a solution, 35-38.

double helix ⊙ the structure formed by two strands of DNA wrapped around each other, 63.

electrode (ē-lek'-trōd) ⊙ the piece of a pH meter that is placed in a solution to detect the pH; sometimes made of glass, 23.

hydrogen (hī'-drə-jən) ⊙ the first element in the periodic table with the symbol H. It has only one proton, one electron, and no neutrons, 5.

hydroxide (hī-dräk'-sīd) ion ⊙ one hydrogen atom and one oxygen atom bonded together, 16, 26.

indicator ⊙ (see acid-base indicator)

ion (ī'-ən) ⊙ an atom that has gained or lost an electron and has a negative or positive electric charge, 36.

ionic (ī-ä'-nik) bond ⊙ a chemical bond in which the electrons are not shared, but one atom donates electrons to the other atom, 11, 36.

kinesin (ki-nē'-sin) ⊙ a protein molecule that is used to carry a cargo down a microtubule "road" to various parts of the cell, 59-60.

lead ⊙ [plumbum, L.] element number 82 in the periodic table with the symbol Pb; has 82 protons, 82 electrons, and 125 neutrons, 4.

liquid state ⊙ the fluid state of a substance, 42.

litmus paper ⊙ an acid-base indicator, 23.

mass ⊙ the property that makes matter resist being moved; commonly, the weight of a substance or object, 3.

matter ⊙ a general term for the stuff that makes up both living and nonliving things, 2.

Mendeleev (men-də-lā'-əf), Dmitri Ivanovich (dmē-trē ē-vän-u-vich) ⊙ first scientist to organize the elements into an arrangement that later became the periodic table of elements, 4, 6.

micelles (mī-celz') ⊙ the small droplets of oil and soap in a water solution, 38.

microtubule (mī-krō-tü'-byül) ⊙ a molecular road inside cells that kinesin uses to move "cargo," 59.

mineral oil ⊙ [octadecane], a material that can be used to dissolve oily substances, 37.

mixture ⊙ two or more substances that are combined, 33-38.

molecule (mä'-li-kyül) ⊙ the product of two or more atoms put together with bonds, 9.

monomer (mä'-nə-mər) ⊙ [mono, one, Gr.; meros, part or unit, Gr.] a molecule that is the individual unit of a polymer, 53.

monosaccharide (mä-nō-sa'-kə-rīd) ⊙ [mono, single, Gr.; saccharide, sugar, Gr.] any of a number of compounds that is a single sugar, 47.

negative charge ⊙ when an atom has gained an electron and thus has more electrons than protons, it has a negative charge, 36.

neutral (nü'-trəl) ⊙ a solution that is neither acidic nor basic, 21.

neutralization (nü-trə-li-zā'-shən) reaction ⊙ another name for an acid-base reaction, 21, 26-27.

neutralize (nü'-trə-līz) ⊙ to use an acid-base reaction to change an acidic or basic solution to one that is neither acidic nor basic, 26-27.

neutron (nü'-trän) ⊙ one of the three fundamental particles that make atoms. It has an atomic mass of 1 and carries no charge—it is "neutral," 3, 5.

nitrogen (nī'-trə-jən) ⊙ the seventh element in the periodic table with the symbol N; has 7 protons, 7 electrons, and 7 neutrons, 12.

noble gases ⊙ the group of elements on the far right-hand side of the periodic table. These elements do not react easily with other elements, 6.

nucleic (nü-klā'-ik) acid bases ⊙ adenine (A), guanine (G), cytosine (C), and thymine (T); the part of DNA that makes the genetic code, 62-63.

nucleotide (nü'-klē-ə-tīd) ⊙ the monomer unit for DNA; made of nucleic acid bases and ribose sugars, 62, 64.

nucleus (nü'-klē-əs) ⊙ the central portion of an atom that houses the protons and neutrons, 3.

nutrients (nü'-trē əntz) ○ substances required by our bodies to stay healthy, 46.

octadecane (äk-tə-de'-kān) ○ mineral oil, 37.

oligosaccharide (ä-li-gō-sa'-kə-rīd) ○ [*oligo*, few, Gr., *saccharide*, sugar, Gr.] any of a number of compounds that are made of a few single sugars, such as sucrose (table sugar), 47.

oxygen (äk'-si-jən) ○ the eighth element in the periodic table; has the symbol O and has 8 protons, 8 electrons, and 8 neutrons, 4, 12.

pH ○ a term used to describe the acidity or basicity of a solution, 21-24.

pH meter ○ an electronic device that detects and displays the pH of a solution, 23.

pH paper ○ a special paper that changes color when placed in either an acid or a base; for example, litmus paper, 23.

paper chromatography ○ a way of separating mixtures by standing a strip of paper in a solution, 43.

peptide (pep'-tīd) bond ○ the attachment between two amino acids connected through the carbonyl group and the amine group, 58.

peptide unit ○ an amino acid in a protein, 58.

periodic table of elements ○ a chart categorizing all of the chemical elements, 4-6.

phenolphtalein (fē-nəl-thā'-lēn) ○ an acid-base indicator; above pH 9 it is pink, below pH 9 it is clear, 24.

plastic ○ any substance made of polyethylene or other similar polymers, 52-53.

plot ○ the graphical representation of data, 29.

polyethylene (pä-lē-e'-thə-lēn) ○ a polymer chain that makes many different plastics, 53.

polymer (pä'-lə-mər) ○ [*poly,* many, Gr; *meros,* part, Gr.] a general term for a molecule having a long chain of many smaller repeating molecular units, 52.

polymerase ○ (see DNA polymerase)

polypeptide (pä-lē-pep'-tīd) ○ a chain of many (but less than 50) peptide units; usually less than a complete protein, 58.

polysaccharide (pä-lē-sa'-kə-rīd) ○ [*poly,* many, Gr.; *saccharide,* sugar, Gr.] any of a number of molecules that are made of many single sugars; for example, starches and cellulose, 48, 52.

pores ○ the small holes that are in a filter, 41.

positive charge ○ when an atom has lost an electron and thus has more protons than electrons, it has a positive charge, 36.

precipitates (pri-si'-pə-tātz) ○ the products of a chemical reaction that are not able to dissolve in the remaining solution and can look like mud, sand, snow, etc., 18.

protein (prō'-tēn) ○ a nutrient; a polymer of amino acids, 46, 57-62.

proton (prō'-tän) ○ one of the three fundamental particles that make atoms. It has an atomic mass of 1 and carries a positive charge, 3-5.

"R" group ○ the group of atoms in an amino acid that makes it unique. The "R" group can be anything from a single hydrogen atom to a complicated ring of atoms, 57.

reaction ○ (see chemical reaction)

ribose (rī'-bōs) ○ a sugar found in DNA nucleotides, 62.

saccharide (sa'-kə-rīd) ○ [Gr., *saccharide,* sugar] a sugar, 47.

salt ○ a product of an acid-base reaction, 26.

salt, table ○ (see sodium chloride)

separation ○ the process of removing one or more items from a mixture, 41.

shared electron bond ◉ (see covalent bond)

sieve ◉ (see filter)

side chains (branches) ◉ atoms that dangle off the main backbone of a polymer and affect its properties 53.

soap ◉ a molecule with a charged end (head) and a long uncharged end (tail). Soap can be dissolved in both water and oily substances and is used for cleaning for this reason, 38.

sodium (sō'-dē-əm) ◉ [natrium, L.] the eleventh element on the periodic table with the symbol Na. It has 11 protons, 11 electrons, and 12 neutrons. Sodium is an alkali metal and combines with chlorine to make sodium chloride (table salt), 4, 15, 16.

sodium bicarbonate (sō'-dē-əm bī-kär'-bə-nāt) ◉ [NaCO$_3$H] baking soda, 21, 26.

sodium chloride (sō'-dē-əm klôr'-īd) ◉ the molecule that results when sodium atoms and chloride atoms are bonded together; table salt, 11, 15.

solid state ◉ the state of a substance when it is in a solid form, such as ice, and has a definite size and shape, 42.

solution (sə-lü'-shen) ◉ a mixture in which one substance has been dissolved in another, 21-22, 27.

solvent (säl'-vənt) ◉ any substance in which another substance is dissolved, 43.

spontaneous (spän-tā'-nē-əs) reaction ◉ when a chemical reaction proceeds without added energy input, 17.

starches ◉ polysaccharides that are found in both plants and animals; provide energy for our bodies 48.

stomach acid ◉ hydrochloric acid [HCl], 22.

sucrose (sü'-krōs) ◉ common table sugar; a disaccharide made of glucose and fructose, 47.

symbol ◉ a unique symbol given to each chemical element. It is usually the first one or two letters of the element name, 4.

T ◉ the symbol for thymine, 62, 63.

table salt (see sodium chloride)

thymine (thī'-mēn) [T] ◉ one of the four nucleic acid bases that make DNA, 62.

titration (tī-trā'-shən) ◉ the experimental technique used to find out the unknown concentration of an acid or a base by use of a neutralization reaction, 28, 30.

tungsten ◉ [wolfram, German] element number 74 in the periodic table with the chemical symbol W. Tungsten has 74 protons, 74 electrons, and 110 neutrons, 4.

unshared electron bond ◉ (see ionic bond)

uranium (yü-rā'-nē-əm) ◉ element number 92 in the periodic table with the chemical symbol U. Uranium has 92 protons, 92 electrons, and 146 neutrons, 5.

vegetable oil ◉ [glycerol trioleate] made of three long chains of hydrogen and carbon atoms hooked together; is not charged, 37.

vinegar ◉ a dilute solution of acetic acid, 21-22, 26-27.

vitamins ◉ nutrients found in foods; required for the healthy functioning of living things, 46.

vulcanization (vul-kə-ni-zā'-shən) ◉ the process by which high heat and sulfur are used to change the properties of sticky natural rubber into a more usable form, 54.

water ◉ [H$_2$O] the molecule formed by two hydrogen atoms and one oxygen atom, 12.

Pronunciation Key

a	add	i	it	p	pit
ā	race	ī	ice	r	run
ä	palm	j	joy	s	sea
â(r)	air	k	cool	sh	sure
b	bat	l	love	t	take
ch	check	m	move	u	up
d	dog	n	nice	ü	sue
e	end	ng	sing	v	vase
ə	a in above	o	odd	w	way
ē	tree	ō	open	y	yarn
f	fit	ô	jaw	z	zebra
g	go	oi	oil		
h	hope	oo	pool		

CPSIA information can be obtained at www.ICGtesting.com
Printed in the USA
LVIW01n2259300517
536378LV00005B/25